THE⊛GRINDERY

Business Booster Workbook

A product of TheGrindery.org
Revision 1
© 2015 The Vision Development Center

by
Willis Bright
George Crawford
Sam Griffin
Corrie Horan
H. Beecher Hicks, III
Dr. Ivan Hicks
John McDonald
Wayne Patrick

This workbook belongs to:

Introduction 5

Welcome 7

Being an Entrepreneur 9
   Objectives...9
   Introduction to Entrepreneurship..9
   Key Traits of an Entrepreneur 10
   The Entrepreneurial Core 11
   Self Evaluation 11

The Core Idea 13
   Objectives...13
   What is a Value Proposition? 13

Building a Business Plan 15
   Objectives...15
   Introduction 15
   What is a business plan?..15
   Why write a business plan?..17
   How to build a business plan 19

Building a Business Network 25
   Objectives...25
   Introduction 25
   Why Do You Network?..25
   Where do You Build Your Network? 26
   Networking Fundamentals 26
   Maintaining and Sustaining Your Network 26
   Ten Commandments of Networking 27
   Sample Networking Questions 27

Financial Basics 29
   Objectives...29
   Introduction 29
   Purpose of Financial Statements...29
   Primary Financial Statements 30
   The Balance Sheet 30
   The Income Statement 34

Marketing Your Brand 39
   Objectives...39
   What Is Branding and Why Is It Important? 39
   Who Are You and How Do You Want To Be Perceived?...39
   Social Media: Brand 40
   Creating Brand Ambassadors...40
   Social Media: Ambassadors 40
   Communicate Your Brand to The Public...41
   Social Media: Communicate 41
   Get Your Target Customers to Amplify Your Brand..42

Funding Your Business..**43**
Objectives..*43*
Introduction...*43*
Types of Business Funding...*43*

Sharing Your Idea..**49**
Objectives..*49*
Introduction...*49*
Value Proposition..*49*
Easy Speech Preparation...*50*
Principles of Public Speaking...*53*

Appendix A: Being an Entrepreneur Worksheet...**57**
Personal Characteristics...*57*
Demands of Owning Your Own Business...*57*
Business Experience and Management Skills..*58*
Self Analysis..*58*
Expectations...*61*

Appendix B: The Core Idea Worksheet...**63**
Value Proposition - State Your Own..*63*
My Competitors - List Your Competitors..*63*
Who Are Your Customers?...*65*
How Do You Find Your Customers?..*65*

Appendix C: Building a Business Plan Worksheet..**67**
Sequoia Capital Business Plan Format..*67*
The Business Model Canvas by Alexander Osterwalder......................................*68*

Appendix D: Building a Business Network Worksheet.......................................**71**

Appendix E: Financial Basics Worksheet...**73**
Balance Sheet..*73*
Income Statement...*74*

Appendix F: Marketing Your Brand Worksheet..**75**

Appendix G: Sharing Your Idea Worksheet...**77**

Notes...**79**

Introduction

The Grindery is one of the first major projects of The Vision Development Center. The Vision Development Center, a 501(c)(3) not-for-profit corporation, initiated through collaboration with organizations such as the MBRA, The Flanner House, First Baptist Church North Indianapolis and CloudOne, is designed establish and operate a urban business development hub.

The Grindery was born out of the need to help people create business enterprise to improve their life chances and life possibilities. The Grindery is intentional about surrounding not just entrepreneurs, but other individuals and organizations as well, with excellent resources and relationships to bring vision to reality.

Students in our courses are challenged to first discover their individual purpose in life, before they are challenged to master coursework individually tailored to create a strong plan for the establishment of their businesses.

Our curriculum design is the result of a pilot experiment done in partnership with Marian University School of Business and early clients of the Center including Christian Theological Seminary, The Efroymson Center at Butler University, and Wells Fargo, helping to develop the UrbanLIFT community grant program.

Welcome

Dear Grinders:

Welcome to The Grindery.

You are officially starting a journey that at times will be stressful, trying, and exhausting. At the same time with every small success it will be exciting, rewarding, and truly fell like an adventure of a lifetime.

We want to reassure you that though this will not be an easy journey, you are surrounded with a team of staff workers and mentors at The Grindery that are here to guide you through these ups and downs. Most of all, we are here to encourage you and cheer you on.

God's blessings to you on this endeavor.

The Grindery Team
http://thegrindery.org

Being an Entrepreneur

Objectives

In this module, you will learn:
- The key traits of an entrepreneur
- The entrepreneurial core
- How to self evaluate

Introduction to Entrepreneurship

Nolan Bushnell founded a company in 1969 to create a home version of an early computer game that ran only on large midrange computers. His product, *Pong*, and his company, Atari, went on to create the home video game industry through the groundbreaking Atari 2600 video game console. After selling the company to Warner Communications in 1978, he launched the Chuck E. Cheese chain of pizza and entertainment restaurants, and formed Catalyst Technologies, a venture capital company. Among other successes, Catalyst funded a major portion of a company called Etak in 1984, which developed the first digitized maps of the world, ultimately providing the core data for MapQuest.com and Google Maps.

It's unlikely that Nolan would have achieved these successes alone – there were many partners, business associates and employees that contributed to these successes. But it's equally unlikely that Nolan would have succeeded if he sat around dreaming and wishing and waiting for something to happen.

Said differently, you have a 100% chance of failure if you do nothing at all.

> *"The critical ingredient is getting off your butt and doing something. It's as simple as that. A lot of people have ideas, but there are few who decide to do something about them now. Not tomorrow. Not next week. But today. The true entrepreneur is a doer, not a dreamer"*
>
> ~ Nolan Bushnell

Key Traits of an Entrepreneur

There are some unique characteristics exhibited by many entrepreneurs. Not all of them are required, but the more you embody, the higher the likelihood of success. The business and financial consulting company, Ernst and Young, lists them as follows:

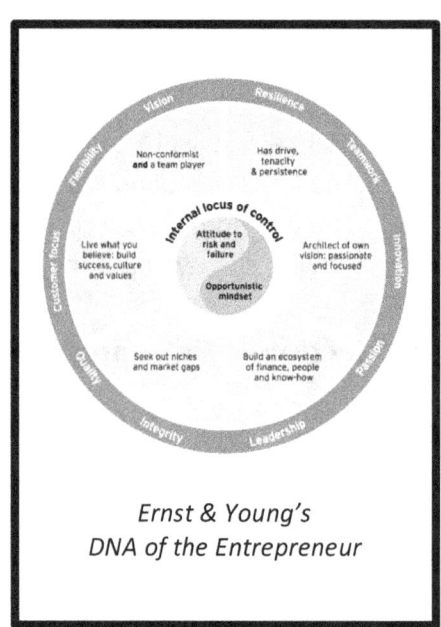

Ernst & Young's
DNA of the Entrepreneur

1. **Drive, Tenacity and Persistence:** An entrepreneur has a stamina that will endure long after all others fade away.
2. **Architect of Vision:** Has a passionate focus on a goal, which is as clear and real to the entrepreneur as anything.
3. **Builds an Ecosystem of Know-How**: An entrepreneur realizes that other people are better at most tasks, and so he or she recruits, delegates and supports them
4. **Seeks out Niches**: There is a constant drive to look for underserved markets, openings or gaps in strategy, or places where a market is not being served
5. **Lives Core Values**: Seeks to maintain core values and integrity, and build a culture around those values
6. **Non Conformist but also a Team Player**: Entrepreneurs are strong team members and cheerleaders for their team, but they don't conform to group think or the status quo. They often look for counter positions to the normal thinking, and then work to build consensus around the position.

The Entrepreneurial Core

Though the above are exhibited characteristics of an entrepreneur, there is a solid core to each one, made up of a set of interesting basic values:

1. **Opportunistic Mindset:** Where others see disruption and chaos, entrepreneurial leaders see opportunity.
2. **Acceptance of Risk and Potential Failure:** Most people avoid risks. Many companies won't take risks until they are about to fail, which is why they are venerable to nimble, smaller competitors. Those companies are usually led by entrepreneurs more willing to take risks.
3. **Internal Focus of Control:** All people wish to be in control of their lives, but entrepreneurs have an internal drive and stamina to act on the urge for control and independence, with a sense of urgency sustained over time.

Self Evaluation

An honest self-evaluation will allow you to assess your personal characteristics and determine your willingness to meet the demands of owning your own business. It is critical to evaluate your personal weaknesses along with your strengths. When owner weaknesses are identified, partners, managers, staff members, other external resources or education and training may be found to balance strengths and offset weaknesses. You'll find a guide to self-evaluation in **Appendix A** of this workbook. Fill it out now if you have not already.

Understanding your personal characteristics, required business skills, and demands of business ownership are critical in helping you find the business best suited to you and your interest. Honestly assessing yourself will help you determine what you need to do to acquire the skills you need, clarify your expectations, and motivate you to seek ways to keep learning as you proceed to develop your business idea.

The Core Idea

Objectives
In this module you will learn:
- What is a Value Proposition?

What is a Value Proposition?
- Value Proposition is the first phase of an effective market opportunity assessment.
- Your Inspiration could be:
  - Where you spend money
  - Source of pain or discomfort in your life, and/or
  - an inefficiency at work
- Identify customer benefits.
- Generally includes statements of:
  - better pricing
  - convenience and/or
  - higher quality product or service
- Put yourself in your customers "shoes".

Most people think first of what they want to express or make then find the audience for their idea. You must work the opposite angle, thinking first of the public. You need to keep your focus on their changing needs, the trends that are washing through them. Beginning with their demand, you create the appropriate supply.

Articulate how your product or service will deliver this value. What mechanisms will you put in place to achieve these results? Then map the basis for differentiation or market play.

Building a Business Plan

Objectives

In this module you'll learn:
- What is a business plan?
- Why write a business plan?
- How to build a business plan

Introduction

A business plan is like the construction plans and architectural blueprints for building a house. The foundation should be in place before framing the walls, and the walls have to be up before raising the roof. In order to figure out how much material to buy and how to fit everything together, the dimensions are required on the blueprints to calculate sizes, lengths and volumes. The construction plans also helps the builder figure out time tables and schedules. Paint should be on site before the painters arrive; pipes, fittings and fixtures before the plumbers arrive; electrical wire before the electricians arrive. In this analogy, the house is like your business, but the construction plans and architectural blueprints are like your business plan. Most importantly, in this class, you are the architect.

What is a business plan?

Wikipedia defines a business plan as "*a formal statement of business goals, reasons they are attainable, and plans for reaching them.*" It's like an architect's blueprints and plans for building a house. It helps you describe what your business is, how it will operate, and how you will acquire customers. It helps you see what you need and when you need it. It also describes key elements of your business such as the problem, your solution, the market and your team.

Ideas to consider about your business plan:

- It's the blueprint for your company
- It includes the description of your product/service
- It explains how you will create and manage your business
- It details your plan for marketing, sales, operations, and financials
- It describes your competition and how you will win
- It describes how you will :
    - Transition from an idea into a startup
    - Acquire customers
    - Build your startup into a sustainable business
- It also needs to be quantifiable (includes numbers):
    - Financials
    - Size of the market
    - Evaluate the industry
- It describes why you have the right team at the right time to take advantage of your business opportunity

Why write a business plan?

Imagine that you have $250,000 to buy a house, but instead of buying a pre-existing house, you decide to have a house built. You might talk with a few builders about your ideal home. Would you sign the check to some random guy who said he would "memorize" all your ideas and knows how to build a house, or would you do some research, take a look at a few floor plans, and shop around before making a decision? Maybe you want granite counter tops in the kitchen, a full basement, and an indoor pool. Would you want to know that the pool puts you $50,000 over budget before or after you sign over the check?

A good plan gets everyone on the same page. In the new home analogy, the plan would communicate to the construction team, e.g., plumbers, electricians, carpenters, etc., when, what, where, why, and how to build. It would also lay out the budget and all the costs. Your business plan will communicate to team, investors, partners, banks, employees, and customers, when, what, where and how you operate as a business.

Consider the new home analogy when you need motivation to write your business plan. Your business plan will help you visualize and measure your business. Your business plan will help you answer the when, what, where, why and how of your business. It will also help you answer those questions from people involved in your business, from partners through customers.

Ideas to consider about your business plan:
- It helps you focus and measure your plan to grow and succeed as a business
- It is like a map that shows you
  - Where you are (current state= startup/idea)
  - Where you want to go (future state= sustainable business)
  - And how to get there (plan for success)
- It helps you define the business and your business objectives
- It helps you measure your chances for success
- It lays out how you will operate your business
- It helps you communicate your ideas and your business goals to
  - Partners and advisors to help you grow
  - Investors for financing your business
  - Management team and employees for operations
  - Customers to attract and sustain business
- It also helps you attract
  - Partners and advisors to explain why they should help you
  - Investors to explain why they should invest
  - Management team and employees to explain why they should join you
  - Customers to explain why they should purchase your product/service
- In the long term, it saves time
  - Starting a business without a plan is like building a house without a plan
  - The plan gets everyone involved on the same page

How to build a business plan

There are many business plan formats to choose from, e.g., SBA, BPlans.com, SCORE, etc. When presenting your business plan, you should be familiar with the format that is preferred by your audience. If you are submitting your business plan for investors or competitions, research their prefered format. Also, avoid mistakes that make the business plan confusing. Also, avoid making the business plan too long. Investors usually review many business plans and won't take the time to review a business plan that is too long, i.e., 20 pages is too long.

Considering a concise business plan, I suggest the format from Sequoia Capital, a venture capital firm in California. Sequoia has invested in many familiar businesses,, e.g., Atari, Cisco, Electronic Arts, EverNote, Oracle, Airbnb, Google, Yahoo, Instagram, YouTube, and more.

Your Company Purpose
- Define the company/business in a single declarative sentence.

Sequoia suggests starting the 1st section of your business plan with the **Company Purpose**. Start with your elevator pitch, and try to distill your elevator pitch into one sentence. This might seem difficult, but imagine this scenario. You attend a networking event and you happen to be on an elevator with Jack Dorsey, CEO of Twitter. You impress Jack with your elevator pitch during the ride up to the top floor, he hands you his card and tells you to send him a tweet to follow up. Now, you only have 140 characters to describe your pitch. What do you do?

The Problem

- Describe the pain of the customer (or the customer's customer).
- Outline how the customer addresses the issue today.

After describing your business in one sentence, introduce the **Problem**. Consider what your customer is currently doing, buying, or feeling. Why or where there is a problem for your customer? What is your customer's pain? Base this section on facts, not just your assumptions.

Your Solution

- Demonstrate your company's value proposition to make the customer's life better.
- Show where your product physically sits.
- Provide use cases.

The third section to include is your **Solution**. Describe how your product or service is a painkiller or gain creator with respect to the customer's problem. This is the section to include your value proposition. Use Appendix B of this workbook to build the Value Proposition into your business plan.

Why Now

- Set-up the historical evolution of your category.
- Define recent trends that make your solution possible.

Next describe **Why Now**. Why is now the right time to solve the customers problem. You want your audience to understand that the opportunity is now.

Market size

- Identify/profile the customer you cater to.
- Calculate the TAM (top down), SAM (bottoms up) and SOM.

Next, describe the your **Market Size** in terms of the number of customer and dollars. You will explain who your customer is, where they are, and how many are experiencing the problem. Many business plans make the mistake of concentrating on an entire industry, e.g., there are 253 million cars and trucks on U.S. roads, or there are 5.3 billion mobile phones in the world. Although knowledge of the industry is important, you should describe your customer archetype, or, in other words, your ideal customer, e.g., there are 100 men under the age of 35 that drive purple cars in the 46208 zip code, or there are 125 women that are 65 or older that play Candy Crush on their smartphone that live near the Grindery.

Competition

- List competitors
- List competitive advantages

The sixth section should describe your **Competition**. How many competitors do you have? What does your competition sale or provide? How much does the competition's product or service cost? How does your competition acquire customers? How many customers does your competition have? Also, for every competitor, be sure to list the advantages or disadvantages for your product or service versus the competition.

Your Product

- Product line-up (form factor, functionality, features, architecture, intellectual property).
- Development roadmap.

This section describes your **Product or Service**. This is where you get into the details of your product or service. If you have a product, you want to include a picture, diagram or illustration of the product. You want to describe the fit, form and function of your product. If you have a service, you want to describe what your service is, when you will provide that service, and how you will deliver the service to the customer. You should also discuss any intellectual property, e.g., patents, trademarks or copyrights that you have developed.

Your Business model

- Revenue model
- Pricing
- Average account size and/or lifetime value
- Sales & distribution model
- Customer/pipeline list

The **Business model** is a representation of your business, how it operates and generates sales to customers. It helps your audience understand your business in context of other existing businesses. Some examples of business models are Brick and Mortar, Direct Sales, Franchising, or Freemium. During your **Market** and **Competition** research, you will find information regarding the Industry that describes your business. Your Industry, Market and Competition will have data regarding how it makes money (Revenue Model) as well as cost for products and services (Pricing). You will also learn how to reach the customer (Sales and distribution model) and generate leads (Customer/pipeline list). The Lean Startup approach that suggests that you get out of the building and interview potential customers. In this way you can test your ideas against what real customers want. Also, the Business Model Canvas model includes the aspects of your business model that could be included in your business plan.

Your Team

- Founders & Management
- Board of Directors/Board of Advisors

Your **Team** includes you, your partners, management and advisors. Since this might be your initial startup, you might be new to this process. You can reinforce your inexperience by describing the experience of your advisors. Include the people in your network that have agreed to partner with you and your business. You should consider including the Grindery in this section.

Your Financials

- P&L
- Balance sheet
- Cash flow
- Cap table
- The deal

Aspects of the **Financials** have many different names, but the four primary financial statements used by all business are the Balance Sheet, the Income Statement, the Statement of Cash Flows, and the Statement of Retained Earnings. The purpose of the Balance Sheet is to give a summary financial position of the company on a specific date. It acts like a "freeze frame" or still picture of a given moment in a company's history. The purpose of the Income statement is to show a company's operations over a period of time. This is in contrast to the balance sheet, which is focused only on a single moment. It accumulates totals of money that flow in and out of a company over the period covered by the statement. The Statement of Cash Flows works in concert with the Income Statement to detail parts of how money is flowing in and out of a business, and the Statement of Retained Earnings works in concert with the Balance Sheet to detail money that is kept for the benefit of shareholders. Use Appendix E of this workbook to develop the Income statement and Balance sheet for your business plan.

Building a Business Network

Objectives

In this module you'll learn:
- Why do you network?
- Where do you build your network?
- Networking Fundamentals
- Maintaining and Sustaining your Network
- The 10 Commandments of Networking
- Sample networking questions

Introduction

Networking is the systematic process of talking to friends, business associates and other contacts about what you are doing or want to do to develop relationships and gather data and information to help you achieve your goals and objectives. It also includes, and is very important for you, to help others achieve their goals and objectives. Networking is:

- Essential to your success
- A two-way street
- A continual and constant process
- Something that works best and needs to happen before you need it.
- 80% communication skills and 20% what you know

Why Do You Network?

1. Gather information and insights
2. Develop strategic relationships and partners
3. Obtain access to decision makers or experts
4. Market and broadcast information about yourself and your business/opportunity

Where do You Build Your Network?

- People
- Events
  - Selection
  - Preparation
  - Participation
- Social Media/Digital Strategies
- Organizations

Networking Fundamentals

- Image is critical
- People/communication skills are very important
- Craft your introduction
  - Simple and direct
  - Clear and concise
  - Results focused
- Develop a goal for each networking activity
  - Be prepared with an ask
  - Determine how many people you can help
  - Determine how many contacts you need to develop
- Networking conversation
  - Avoid gossip
  - Positive attitude
  - Be authentic
  - Find common ground
  - Explain exactly how that person can help you
  - Determine how you can help them

Maintaining and Sustaining Your Network

- Follow up
- Prioritizing
- Helping others

Ten Commandments of Networking

1. Have your networking tools with you at all times (business cards, mints, etc.)
2. Set goals on the number of people you will/want to meet
3. Act like a host not a guest
4. Exchange business cards with people you meet
5. Listen and ask the 5 W's: who, what, why, where, when
6. Write comments on the back of cards you gather
7. Give a lead or referral whenever possible
8. Describe your product or service quickly - under 2 minutes
9. Keep circulating - don't linger
10. Follow up with your contacts

---

10 Commandments of Networking

Tools
Goals
Host
Exchange
Listen
Comments
Leads
Describe
Circulate
Follow Up

Sample Networking Questions

- You are an authority or expert in my target area can you tell me something about…?
- How do you see the climate or state of your industry/area?
- Where is your industry going in the future?
- Who are the key people or organizations in your industry?
- What companies are well managed and doing well?
- What companies are growing?
- What do your customers tell you their needs are going to be in the next five years?
- What changes do you see happening in your industry/field in the next 5 years?
- What are the major problems you are facing?
- What is the culture of your company/industry?
- What organizations are important in your industry?
- What other people do you think I should talk to about your industry?
- What is the best way for you and me to develop a relationship?
- What can I do to help you?

Financial Basics

Objectives

In this module you'll learn:
- The purpose of Financial Statements
- Primary Financial Statements
- The Balance Sheet
- The Income Statement

Introduction

The purpose of a for-profit business is to make money for the owners of the business. The purpose of a non-profit business is to generate enough revenue to cover the costs of the business, with as close to zero left over as possible. In both cases, knowing how much money is coming in (and from what sources), and where it is going out is probably the most important function of a business owner. All too often well-meaning prospective business owners believe they can ignore or leave to others (like accountants) the financial fundamentals of their business, but usually those people become former business owners very quickly!

Purpose of Financial Statements

Although you may know your business "like the back of your hand," the primary purpose of financial statements is to share, in a uniform way, key financial data about how your business is operating and what condition its in. This can be useful for any number of reasons, including raising capital funds from investors, seeking to secure a loan, obtaining credit from a supplier, or educating employees about their part of the business. Some core questions that are answered by financial statements include:

- What is the company's current financial status?
- What was the company's operating results for the period?
- How did the company obtain and use cash during the period?

Primary Financial Statements

There are four primary financial statements used by all businesses. They are:

- The Balance Sheet
- The Income Statement
- The Statement of Cash Flows
- The Statement of Retained Earnings

In this module, we will focus on the Balance Sheet and the Income Statement. The Statement of Cash Flows works in concert with the Income Statement to detail parts of how money is flowing in and out of a business, and the Statement of Retained Earnings works in concert with the Balance Sheet to detail money that is kept for the benefit of shareholders.

The Balance Sheet

The purpose of the Balance Sheet is to give a summary financial position of the company on a specific date. It acts like a "freeze frame" or still picture of a given moment in a company's history. It has three primary sections:

- **Assets**: anything of value that a company owns, including cash, accounts receivable, inventory, land, buildings, equipment and intangible items.
- **Liabilities**: anything that a company owes to others, or reduces the value of an asset, including accounts payable, loans and notes payable, and mortgages payable
- **Equity**: What remains of the assets after all obligations are satisfied.

The core equation of the balance sheet is:

Equity = Assets – Liabilities

Usually this is reordered on a balance sheet to be:

Assets = Liabilities + Equity

> The balance sheet must always balance. Assets always equal liabilities + equity. This means that if liabilities are greater than assets, the company will have **negative equity**. If the company were to cease operations, it would be considered **bankrupt**, and the owners would have no assets to distribute.

When presented, a Balance Sheet generally lists all assets, then all liabilities, then the amount of equity. The assets always equal the liabilities plus the equity – they are always in balance – hence the name, Balance Sheet.

Below is a sample balance sheet:

Balance Sheet
JK Enterprises
As of January 31, 2015

Assets

Cash & Equivalents	$40.00
Accounts Receivable	$100.00
Land	$200.00
Total Assets	$340.00

Liabilities

Accounts Payable	$50.00
Notes Payable	$150.00
Total Liabilities	$200.00

Equity

Capital Stock	$100.00
Retained Earnings	$40.00
Total Equity	$140.00
Total Liabilities and Equity	$340.00

Here are the key parts of the sample balance sheet:

- **Assets include all things of value that the business owns**, including the cash they have on hand, and the value of the land they own.

- **Accounts Receivable is money owed to the company by others**, which could include products or services sold that have not yet been paid for.

- **Accounts Payable is money owed by the company to others**, which could include raw materials received but not yet paid for, or any sort of bill that the company has yet to pay.

- **Notes Payable is the amount of outstanding loans that are due**. These reduce the value of the assets. For example, the land may be worth $200, but if $150 still remains on a loan used to purchase it, the net value is $50, which is $200 - $150. Both parts of the are listed on the balance sheet – value of the land or object as an asset, and the amount of the loan balance remaining as a liability. Nearly every asset that has some sort of loan against it is reflected in this balanced way.

- **Capital Stock is money invested in the company**. When a company sells part of the ownership of a company to others, it sells "shares" of the company. The amount received for these shares is listed as Capital Stock, and reflects the amount of money owed back to those shareholders when they want to sell their shares in the company.

- **Retained Earnings is all the money collected by the company to the benefit of shareholders**. When a company spends less than it makes, it is said to make a "profit". If the profits aren't immediately sent out to shareholders (which is called a "dividend") and kept in a bank account, they are reflected as Retained Earnings. It represents the growth in the value of the company since the shares were sold.

> Investors in a company purchase "shares" of a company, which measure the amount of a company owned by any given investor. If those shares are traded in open markets, such as the New York Stock Exchange, the company is said to be a **Public** company. If they are only owned by a specific group of people and aren't traded in an exchange, it is said they are a **Private** company.

The equity and liabilities added together in this example equal the assets, so the Balance Sheet is balanced. There are, however, some limitations of balance sheets:

- **Assets are recorded at their historical value.** When an asset is acquired or purchased, the value of that asset goes on the balance sheet, and any liens or loans against it do as well (as liabilities). But the value of many assets decreases over time, a process called "depreciation". Depreciation of assets isn't captured on a balance sheet with the asset, so it can give a viewer a false impression of the value of assets if many have depreciated.

- **Only recognizes assets that can be expressed in monetary terms.** There are many assets of a business that don't translate easily into a monetary value, such as the "feeling" a people have when they do business with you (called "goodwill") or the value of the brand or logo of a company. Although accountants work to capture the value of these assets anyway, it is an imprecise measurement and can greatly inflate or deflate the value of these non-monetary assets.

> Goodwill is often accumulated over time based on years of positive public views of a company, but can also be decreased as an asset when there is a negative event in the company's life, such as a major product recall or a scandal involving its leadership.

- **Equity doesn't reflect the market value.** The equity portion of the balance sheet records only money obtained from the sale of the stock, as well as any profits not distributed to shareholders and kept by the company (as retained earnings). The value of a company, though, is rarely simply the total of these two numbers. For example, technology companies that intentionally lose money by applying money obtained from stock sales to increased sales and marketing activities or product development frequently record a <u>negative</u> equity amount – but are worth significantly more in the market than the balance sheet reflects.

The Income Statement

The purpose of the income statement is to show a company's operations over a period of time. This is in contrast to the balance sheet, which is focused only on a single moment. It accumulates totals of money that flow in and out of a company over the period covered by the statement. It, like the balance sheet, has three primary sections:

- **Revenues**: any assets (especially cash) that are created through business operations

- **Expenses**: any assets (especially cash) that are consumed through business operations

- **Net Income (or loss)**: what remains after all expenses are deducted from all revenues.

Like the balance sheet, the Income statement also has a core formula:

Revenue – Expenses = Net Income (or Loss)

Companies are said to make a **Profit** if net income is positive (revenue is greater than expenses). They are said to have produced a **Loss** if net income is negative (expenses are greater than revenue).

The next page has a sample income statement. Note that there are two columns in the statement, describing events for two separate years. This is because it's often useful to compare time periods on financial statements to understand the general trend of a business.

It is always helpful to have income statements and balance sheets that represent multiple years of activity. The trends observed are often more important than the raw numbers in any given period.

Income Statement

JK Enterprises

For Years Ended December 31 2013 and 2014

	2013	2014
Revenue		
Sales	$100.00	$85.00
Other Revenue	$30.00	$15.00
Total Revenue	$130.00	$100.00
Expenses		
Cost of Goods Sold	$62.00	$58.00
Sales, General & Administrative	$16.00	$12.00
Research & Development	$8.00	$7.00
Total Expenses	$86.00	$77.00
Earnings Before Interest, Taxes, Depreciation & Amortization	$44.00	$23.00
Income Taxes	$20.00	$18.00
Net Income	$24.00	$5.00

Here are the key parts of the income statement:

- **Revenue**: The assets created through the normal business operations of the company. In this example, these come from **Sales**, which is money generated from selling the product of the company, and **Other Revenue** which is any money collected from sources other than sales.

- **Expenses**: The outflows of company assets to others. In this example these are Cost of Goods Sold and Sales, General & Administrative expenses.

- **Cost of Goods Sold:** This expense totals the money spent to purchase or produce the products sold to the customer, sometimes shortened to **COGS**. Almost all businesses need to pay for the items they sell, either from suppliers or through raw materials that they assemble into their product. Even businesses that sell the time of people, such as services businesses, would often account for the payroll of those people as form of cost of goods sold.

- **Sales, General and Administrative**: These are expenses related to running the business. Generally, they are considered sales, general and administrative (or **SG&A**) expenses if they cannot be attributed to the sale of a specific product or service. Examples are salaries of business leadership, office rent and marketing activities. If it can be aligned to a specific sale, it is generally considered COGS, whereas if it is a generic expense that affects all sales activities, it's SG&A.

- **Research & Development**: Money expended to develop the products of the company. This is much greater in technology-based companies than retail companies, as the value of the product is key to winning sales.

- **Earnings Before Interest, Taxes, Depreciation & Amortization:** Often shortened to **EBITDA**, this measurement is essentially the revenue minus expenses, but before provisions are made for interest, taxes, depreciation and amortization. The significance of EBITDA is that it accounts for all the expenses that are generally in direct control of management of the company. Expenses accounted for after EBITDA is stated generally have accounting-based or contract-based terms that are unchangeable or inflexible to the management team, and so in some ways it's a measurement of management success. Expenses listed after EBITDA are:

  - **Interest**: The amount of money paid to others for having borrowed money. It is essentially the cost of borrowing the money.

  - **Taxes**: Money paid to governments through taxation laws.

  - **Depreciation**: The accumulated reduction in the value of assets of the company. Though assets are listed on the balance sheet, the reduction in value of those assets is considered an expense and is put on the income statement. For example, if you purchased a car for your business for $40,000, five years later the car may only be worth $10,000. The difference in value over this time, $30,000, is called depreciation.

  - **Amortization**: Payments made on any loan or agreement that are spread out over time. For instance, if the business decided to take a loan out to buy the car, the payments would be considered amortization. Amortization can also be used to spread out the costs of non-

> The purpose of EBITDA is to grade management. By pausing on that line of an income statement, it's clear to see how management has controlled (or failed to control) the things that are within their control. The other expenses below EBITDA – Interest, Taxes, Depreciation and Amortization, are largely out of control of management on the short term.

tangible assets – things that have value but are not physical, such as a rebranding of the company or a campaign to increase positive public impressions (goodwill) of the company.

- **Net Income** (or Loss)**:** What remains of revenue after all expenses are paid. If this is a positive number, the company made a profit. If it is negative, it posted a loss.

Many are surprised to learn that a company can intentionally run at a loss (negative net income) intentionally for an extended period of time. During times of loss, the company generally lives on assets, as negative net income reduces the amount of assets available, such as cash in the bank. Companies that have significant assets, such as cash, marketable securities and other sellable assets such as art collections or buildings, can exist for a long time – even decades – while posting losses.

> Net income is often called the "bottom line" as it's the last line in the income statement. It's given rise to the popular cliché, "give me the bottom line", which means to get directly to to the point. **It is the point of a business to produce positive net income.** It is why businesses exist!

Technology companies often are constructed to intentionally lose money in order to increase their customer base in preparation for an eventual sale. In this case, they take investor money and book it as an asset, and then run the business at a loss, spending more money on SG&A (primarily sales efforts and marketing efforts) as well as R&D (to develop the product), which should have the effect of creating more customers quickly for a product with higher value. If they succeed, the company is generally bought by a larger organization who reduces the SG&A and R&D spend down to normal levels, and reaps the benefits of profits made by the acquired organization.

In Appendix E: Financial Basics Worksheet, you'll find a set of blank financial statements where you can attempt to plan for the first two years of your business.

Marketing Your Brand

Objectives

In this module you'll learn:
- What is branding and why is it important?
- Who are you and how do you want to be perceived?
- Using social media for branding
- How to create brand ambassadors
- How to communicate your brand to the public

What Is Branding and Why Is It Important?

- Branding is the marketing practice of creating a name, symbol, or design that identifies differentiates a product from other products.
- Branding is important because it gives you a major edge in increasingly competitive markets.

Who Are You and How Do You Want To Be Perceived?

- Understand the business niche you are in. How are you different from your competitors?
- Know your target audience to the core.
- Fully grasp how your product and services hit the sweet spot of your audience's needs

---

BACK Guidelines

B – Brand
(Figure out what your brand is)

A – Ambassadors
(Create brand ambassadors

C – Communicate
(Communicate to the public)

K – Keep
(Keep the public engaged with your brand)

Social Media: Brand

- Use Google to do a Top 10 search of competitors
- Use social media sites such as Facebook, Twitter, Pinterest, Tumblr, and Blogger to search specific topics pertaining to your industry. This will help you find your target audience. Use hashtags (#).
- Once you find your target audience on these sites take the time to read what people are posting about. Make note of the positive things people are saying, the negative things, and also any suggestions they might have. This could give you a leg up if you can find a way to meet their needs.

Creating Brand Ambassadors

- You as an owner/management have to know your brand, but also be able to convey it to others.
- Include your staff/volunteers as brand ambassadors.
    - Fully capture what your brand equals in an easily digestible format.
    - Train your employees to embody the brand and what it equals. How to display it.
    - Have systems and protocols in place to aid employees in keeping the core of the brand at the top of their mind.

Social Media: Ambassadors

- In the beginning pick one person to manage your social media accounts.
- As you grow your accounts find 10 people you can count on to spread your message.
- As your team grows you can assign one social account to each member.

Communicate Your Brand to The Public

- Devise the manner in which employees should interact with customers.
    - Create phrases/descriptions that hit the mark when communicating with customers or clients.
- Put together a check and balance system to ensure employee to customer messaging stays on brand.
    - Create a checklist of points to touch on when engaging with customers/clients.
    - Create a situational list of customer questions and employee responses.
- Carefully consider your first and last impression you want to make when communicating the brand with the public.
    - Punctuate the brand at the start and finish.
    - First and last impressions are key
    - Lead them to the right path in consumer engagement and help them support the brand.

> **Creating Situational Lists of Customer Questions & Employee Responses**
>
> Keep a record of popular questions you had to answer before you had employees
>
> Use your competition's pages and use their FAQs as a template

Social Media: Communicate

- Make sure you are 100% you/your brand across every social media outlet.
- Make sure your ambassadors are using the same messages across all outlets.
- Be social, interact, answer questions, respond to feedback.

Get Your Target Customers to Amplify Your Brand

- Make sure all communications, individual or mass, are consistent and in line with brand positioning.
- Have one person/group review all outside messaging and any brand associations.
- Reward loyal customers and fans with perks and special treatment to show your appreciation.

Incentives, Incentives, Incentives!

Rewards cards, special online incentives, sales, etc. – people LOVE getting things for free or on discount.

They also just like winning to say they won, which is why contests are an amazing tool to use for both brick-and-mortar stores and your online sites.

Get creative! Think of some of your favorite games you would play and find a way to make them interactive online.

By doing this, you can get people to sign up for your newsletters, text messaging or coupon clubs.

Funding Your Business

Objectives
In this module you'll learn about the pros and cons of the major ways you can fund your business.

Introduction
There are many sources of capital for starting, growing or running a business – more than you may have ever considered. However, one size does not fit all. Each circumstance is unique; and choices should be made carefully.

Alternatives for business funding include:

1. Personal Savings
2. Friends & Family
3. Get a Contract
4. Crowd Funding
5. Get a Partner
6. Credit Cards
7. Angel Financing or Venture Capital
8. Bank Loan
9. Venture Philanthropy

Let's look at each of these options a little more closely.

Types of Business Funding

Personal Savings
In this method, you use your own money to fund your business.

Pros:
- You are in control! It's your budget and your strategy
- You will spend your own money more carefully than others

Cons:

- You don't have the money to invest, or your idea is bigger than your money
- You won't have savings for retirement or emergencies

Friends and Family

The old maxim "Fools rush in where angels fear to tread..." is appropriate for this funding method, because it involves relying on your own family or friends to fund your business.

Pros:
- May be the easiest and fastest source of support
- Cost of funding may be low

Cons:
- Can make for tough dinner conversation

Contracts

In this method of funding, you wait until you have your first contract and then use the proceeds from that to setup the rest of your business functions.

Pros:
- Validates your business and model
- Minimizes the investment required to start
- You maintain control of your equity (stock, ownership)

Cons:
- You pay have to build the product or service first
- You may need more capital faster

Crowd Funding

In this method, you post the need for funding to a website and rely on donations and/or investments from strangers to fund your business.

Pros:
- Seems pretty easy
- Demonstrates buy-in for the idea from the masses
- You can structure the "investment" uniquely

Cons:
- It's not as easy as it looks
- No guarantee of success
- Exposes your business concept broadly

Partnership

In this method, you find another person (or persons) to share the ownership, risk, management and funding of the business.

Pros:
- Your partner(s) may have expertise that you don't
- You bring the "sweat" while they bring the "equity"
- Share in the risk

Cons:
- You have to share in the vision setting and decision making
- Doesn't always work out
- Share in the rewards

Credit Cards

In this method, you use credit card companies as a form of business loan to start your business.

Pros:
- Borrow against your personal credit rating
- Readily available
- Maintain your equity

Cons:
- Credit cards can be **evil**
- Converges personal and business credit ratings

Angel Investors or Venture Capital

In this method, you recruit people (angels) or companies (venture capital) to invest in your business as co-owners to receive funding in the form of stock purchases.

Pros:
- Investors can bring value beyond the capital
- You now have partners
- Plan has to be tight

Cons:
- May be tough to get
- You now have partners
- Plan has to be tight
- May be/seem expensive

Bank Financing

In this method you obtain a loan from a traditional financial institution or bank.

Pros:
- Maintain control of equity
- Reasonable cost of capital

Cons:
- Must have assets (business or personal) to borrow against (collateral)
- Personal guarantees
- Arduous application process

Venture Philanthropy

In this method, you obtain funding from philanthropic people or organizations who wish to give money for social change.

Pros:
- Can help pursue ventures for social good
- Want return in social value vs. money

Cons:
- New phenomenon – not widely available
- Only applies to specific circumstances

Sharing Your Idea

Objectives

In this module you'll learn:
- What a Value Proposition is and how to create one
- How to prepare a speech in simple steps
- The main principles of public speaking

Introduction

Though the primary purpose of a business is to sell products or services for a profit, one of the key jobs a leader of a business must master is how to sell the business itself. Now, that doesn't mean selling the entire business to another company or organization (though that sometimes happens.) What it means is being able to sell others on the value and mission of the business you lead.

You will need these skills for nearly any activity that's related to the development of your business, including recruiting suppliers, hiring people, raising capital for expansion, obtaining loans – and occasionally for a big, important sales opportunity. Of course, someday you may want to sell your business completely, at which point these skills are of the highest importance.

Value Proposition

In The Core Idea, we learned that the value proposition is the first phase of an effective market opportunity assessment, and essentially is the **core problem your business is out to solve** for pay and profit.

Your inspiration could be:
- Where you spend money
- Source of pain or discomfort in your life
- Inefficiency at work

The first step to identifying your value proposition is to clearly **identify the customer benefits**. These are statements that proclaim what your business does different or better to solve needs of a customer, like:

- Better pricing
- More convenience
- Higher quality

Essentially you want to put yourself in your customer's shoes and outline how buying your product and service is better than your competitor.

Secondly, you then need you articulate how **your product or service will deliver this value.** What mechanisms will you put in place to achieve these results?

Lastly, you want to establish your **target**. This is all about mapping the basis for your differentiation or market play.

Easy Speech Preparation

Below is an adaptation of the *Easy Steps to Speech Preparation* as authored by the Westside Toastmasters of Indianapolis.

Establish the Purpose of your Speech

The primary purposes of a speech are to:
- Inform
- Entertain
- Persuade
- Console
- Call the Audience to Action

Research Your Potential Audience

When thinking about your speech, you want to consider these questions about your audience:

- Who will be in the audience?
- Why will they be there?
- What might be their interest?
- What will motivate the people there?

Gather Information to Support Your Purpose

As you prepare your speech, you want to research information that will help you make your point to the audience. The sources of this information could include:

- Trade Publications
- The Internet
- Government Agencies & Regulatory Bodies
- Observations & Study of Your Competition

Create a Clear Purpose Statement

The first thing to write down on the notecards you'll use when you deliver your speech, be it on paper or simply in your head, is to have a clear, sharp and easy to understand purpose statement. It is the main point you are making in your speech, and the one you want everyone to take away with them if they remember nothing else. Consider these guidelines:

- Keep Your Focus Sharp
- Don't Let Your Subject Be Too Broad
- KISS (Keep It Simple, Stupid!)

Construct an Outline

Next you want to arrange all the key proof points you've gathered into a logical arrangement, with main points leading sub points in a form of an outline.

Easy Preparation Steps

1. Write out a **purpose statement**
2. Know your **audience**
3. Gather **proof points**
4. Craft a **purpose statement**
5. Build an **outline** of your proof points.
6. Devise an i**mpactful opening**
7. Write out your **summary and logical conclusion**
8. Write out the rest of the speech and **practice** it
9. Anticipate **questions** and practice your answers in advance

Devise an Opening with Impact

Just like a great book or movie often starts with a jarring image or a scene that sets the mood for the piece, your speech too should begin with something impactful. This could include a little-known fact, a startling statistic, a picture or image or any other device that will grab and hold the listener's attention.

Craft your Summary and Logical Conclusion

These items are at the end of your speech and serve to reiterate the points you've made already in your outline of key points, which followed your impactful opening. You should repeat in most cases what you've already said in simple format, so people walking away from your speech remember your key points.

Write, Edit and Practice the Delivery of your Speech

Now that you've assembled all the key parts – an impactful opening, proof points arranged into a logical outline hierarchy, and a thoughtful summary that repeats many of your key take-away pints – you are ready to write out all you'd like to say by filling in all the blanks between the phrases.

Understand, though, that you don't want to read a speech from pages like a book when you deliver it. The purpose of writing it out is to force you to think about transitions and the logical points of argument you'll deliver as you speak. These transitions and logical flow are what often separates someone considered a "good" speaker from someone who is considered "great."

Anticipate Questions and be Ready to Answer

No matter how carefully you've prepared your material, you're likely to encounter questions at the end of your speech. This time is to be cherished and engaged in whole-heartedly, as it reveals not only where you might need to deepen your material to avoid the question in the future, but also how the audience has received the material. If the questions are deep and thoughtful, you know you've managed to connect with your listeners. If they are shallow and repeat items previously shared, you may have failed to fully help everyone understand your key points. Either way, anticipate potential questions by writing them down along with your intended answers, and then practice answering them as if it were live.

Principles of Public Speaking

Richard Zeoli founded and operates RZC Impact, an executive communications training firm. He's authored the book *The 7 Principles of Public Speaking.* His key ideas for being a good public speaker are below.

1. **Perception: Stop trying to be a great "public" speaker.**
   People want to listen to someone who is interesting, relaxed, and comfortable. In the routine conversations we have every day, we have no problem being ourselves. Yet too often, when we stand up to give a speech, something changes. We focus on the "public" at the expense of the "speaking." To become an effective public speaker, you must do just the opposite: focus on the speaking and let go of the "public." Think of it as a conversation between you and the audience. If you can carry on a relaxed conversation with one or two people, you can give a great speech. Whether your audience consists of two people or two thousand and whether you're talking about the latest medical breakthrough or what you did today at work, be yourself; talk directly to people and make a connection with them.

2. **Perfection: When you make a mistake, no one cares but you.**
   Even the most accomplished public speaker will make a mistake at some point. Just keep in mind that you'll notice more than anyone in your audience. The most important thing a speaker can do after making a mistake is to keep going. Don't stop and—unless the mistake was truly earth shattering—never apologize to the audience for a minor slip. Unless they are reading the speech during your delivery, the audience won't know if you left out a word, said the wrong name, or skipped a page. Because "to err is human," a mistake can actually work for you, because it allows you to connect with your audience. People don't want to hear from someone who is "perfect;" they will relate much more easily to someone who is real.

3. **Visualization: If you can see it, you can speak it.**
   Winners in all aspects of life have this in common: they practice visualization to achieve their goals. Sales people envision themselves closing the deal; executives picture themselves developing new ventures; athletes close their eyes and imagine themselves making that basket, hitting that home run, or breaking that record. The same is true in public speaking. The best way to fight anxiety and to become a more comfortable speaker is to practice in the one place where no one else can see you—your mind. If you visualize on a consistent basis, your mind will become used to the prospect of speaking in public, and pretty soon you'll conquer any feelings of anxiety.

4. **Discipline: Practice makes perfectly good.**
   Your goal is not to be a perfect public speaker. There is no such thing. Your goal is to be an effective public speaker. Like anything else in life, it takes practice. We too often take communication for granted because we speak to people everyday. But when your prosperity is directly linked to how well you perform in front a group, you need to give the task the same attention as if you were a professional athlete. Remember, even world champion athletes practice every day. Try taking a class where you practice giving speeches.

5. **Description: Make it personal.**
   Whatever the topic, audiences respond best when speakers personalize their communication. Take every opportunity to put a face on the facts of your presentation. People like to hear about other people's experiences—the triumphs, tragedies, and everyday humorous anecdotes that make up their lives. Tell stories. Whenever possible, insert a personal-interest element in your public speaking. Not only will it make your listeners warm up to you, but it will also do wonders at putting you at ease. After all, on what subject is your expertise greater than on the subject of you?

6. **Inspiration: Speak to serve.**
   For a twist that is sure to take much of the fear out of public speaking, take the focus off of yourself and shift it to your audience. After all, the objective is not to benefit the speaker but to benefit the audience, through teaching, motivation, or entertainment. So in all of your preparation and presentation, you should think about your purpose. How can you help your audience members achieve their goals?

7. **Anticipation: Always leave 'em wanting more.**
   One of the most valuable lessons I have learned in my years in is that when it comes to public speaking, less is usually more. I don't think I've ever left a gathering and heard someone say, "I wish that speaker had spoken longer." On the other hand, I imagine that you probably can't count the times that you've thought, "I'm glad that speech is over. It seemed to go on forever!" So surprise your audience. Always make your presentation just a bit shorter than anticipated. If you've followed the first six principles outlined here you already have their attention and interest, and it's better to leave your listeners wishing you had spoken for just a few more minutes than squirming in their seats waiting for your speech finally to end.

Appendix A: Being an Entrepreneur Worksheet

Check the questions below that you can answer with "Yes."

Personal Characteristics

- ❏ Are you a leader?
- ❏ Are you confident?
- ❏ Do you like to make your own decisions?
- ❏ Do you handle responsibility well?
- ❏ Do you thoroughly plan projects from start to finish?
- ❏ Are you self-disciplined and independent?
- ❏ Are you flexible?
- ❏ Do you read business publications?
- ❏ Do you possess computer skills?
- ❏ Are you aware of your current credit rating?
- ❏ Are you or your spouse willing to dip into your savings if necessary to help support the business?
- ❏ Will your spouse's income be sufficient to support your family without income from your business?

Demands of Owning Your Own Business

- ❏ Do you realize that running a business may require long hours and reduced personal income?
- ❏ Do you have the emotional strength and good health to handle the workload and daily schedule that owning your own business will require?
- ❏ If required, are you prepared to temporarily lower your standard of living until your business is firmly established?
- ❏ Is your family prepared to support you (time and money required to start a business)?

Business Experience and Management Skills

- ❏ What basic skills do you think you will need to succeed in business?
- ❏ Do you possess those skills?
- ❏ If you discover you do not have the basic skills needed for your business, are you willing to delay your plans until you have acquired the necessary skills?
- ❏ Have you ever worked in a managerial or supervisory position?
- ❏ Have you hired and fired people before?
- ❏ Have you ever worked in a business similar to the one you are considering?
- ❏ Have you had any business training in school?
- ❏ Do you understand business financing and cash flow management?
- ❏ Ae you aware of the record keeping requirements expected in managing a small business?
- ❏ Do you understand the fundamentals of marketing and market development?

Self Analysis

This self-test is simply an overview of the personal characteristics and basic skills needed in small business ownership. The questions with a "Yes" answer indicate the presence of a strength or attribute needed to successfully manage a small business. Those not checked might indicate weaknesses or a lack of willingness to make the sacrifices necessary to run a small business. If you decide to continue with plans to establish a business, then you should resolve to change each blank to a "Yes." A partner or other solution may provide balance for some weak areas, thus changing a few blanks to "Yes." However, if there are a significant number of unchecked boxes, overcoming problems may require more development on your part.

Identify the five most important interests, skills, or previous work experience that you enjoyed:

Write below any opportunities that may be associated with these characteristics, skills, or previous work experience.

Based on your interest, abilities, and experience, summarize your strengths and weaknesses as they relate to the business skills necessary to start and grow a successful business.

My strengths are:

My strengths identified by someone who knows me well are:

My weaknesses are:

My weaknesses identified by someone who knows me well are:

Identify ways you can overcome these weaknesses:

What kind of commitment are you willing to make to get your business off the ground?

Time commitment:

Resources commitment:

Are you prepared to lose your investment and other savings? _____ Yes _____ No

Expectations

What are your expectations for the business:?

Within one year?

After three years?

Appendix B: The Core Idea Worksheet

Value Proposition - State Your Own

Mission Statement:

Product:

Service:

Target:

My Competitors - List Your Competitors

Company Name:

Competitors:

Why are you better?

Who Are Your Customers?

Names of Companies:

Customer Description:

Customer Needs:

How Do You Find Your Customers?

Company Name:

Customers - Where do you find them?

Customer - How do you connect with them?

Appendix C: Building a Business Plan Worksheet

Here is are two different, complete business plan outlines – one from Sequoia Capital and the other by Alexander Osterwalder. As you build your own business plan in a tool such as Microsoft Word or Google Docs, ensure that it contains all of these sections.

Sequoia Capital Business Plan Format
- Company purpose
  - Define the company/business in a single declarative sentence.
- Problem
  - Describe the pain of the customer (or the customer's customer).
  - Outline how the customer addresses the issue today.
- Solution
  - Demonstrate your company's value proposition to make the customer's life better.
  - Show where your product physically sits.
  - Provide use cases.
- Why now
  - Set-up the historical evolution of your category.
  - Define recent trends that make your solution possible.
- Market size
  - Identify/profile the customer you cater to.
  - Calculate the TAM (top down), SAM (bottoms up) and SOM.
- Competition
  - List competitors
  - List competitive advantages
- Product
  - Product line-up (form factor, functionality, features, architecture, intellectual property).
  - Development roadmap.
- Business model
  - Revenue model
  - Pricing
  - Average account size and/or lifetime value
  - Sales & distribution model
  - Customer/pipeline list
- Team
  - Founders & Management
  - Board of Directors/Board of Advisors
- Financials
  - P&L

- o   Balance sheet
- o   Cash flow
- o   Cap table
- o   The deal

The Business Model Canvas by Alexander Osterwalder
- Value Propositions:
  - o   products and services a business offers to meet the needs of its customers.
  - o   what distinguishes itself from its competitors.
  - o   provides value through various elements such as
    - newness,
    - performance,
    - customization,
    - "getting the job done",
    - design,
    - brand/status,
    - price,
    - cost reduction,
    - risk reduction,
    - accessibility,
    - convenience/usability.
  - o   The value propositions may be:
    - Quantitative- price and efficiency
    - Qualitative- overall customer experience and outcome
- Customer Segments:
  - o   Identify which customers you serve.
  - o   Segment various customers based on the different needs
  - o   Ensure your strategy meets the needs of the various customer segments:
    - Mass Market: There is no specific segmentation for a company that follows the Mass Market element as the organization displays a wide view of potential clients. e.g. Car
    - Niche Market: Customer segmentation based on specialized needs and characteristics of its clients. e.g. Rolex
    - Segmented: A company applies additional segmentation within existing customer segment. In the segmented situation, the business may further distinguish its clients based on gender, age, and/or income.
    - Diversify: A business serves multiple customer segments with different needs and characteristics.
    - Multi-Sided Platform / Market: For a smooth day-to-day business operation, some companies will serve mutually dependent customer segment. A credit card company will provide services to credit card holders while simultaneously assisting merchants who accept those credit cards.

- Channels:
  - A company can deliver its value proposition to its targeted customers through different channels.
  - Effective channels will distribute a company's value proposition in ways that are fast, efficient and cost effective.
  - An organization can reach its clients either through its own channels (store front), partner channels (major distributors), or a combination of both.
- Customer Relationships:
  - To ensure the survival and success of any businesses, companies must identify the type of relationship they want to create with their customer segments.
    - Personal Assistance: Assistance in a form of employee-customer interaction. Such assistance is performed either during sales, after sales, and/or both.
    - Dedicated Personal Assistance: The most intimate and hands on personal assistance where a sales representative is assigned to handle all the needs and questions of a special set of clients.
    - Self Service: The type of relationship that translates from the indirect interaction between the company and the clients. Here, an organization provides the tools needed for the customers to serve themselves easily and effectively.
    - Automated Services: A system similar to self-service but more personalized as it has the ability to identify individual customers and his/her preferences. An example of this would be Amazon.com making book suggestion based on the characteristics of the previous book purchased.
    - Communities: Creating a community allows for a direct interaction among different clients and the company. The community platform produces a scenario where knowledge can be shared and problems are solved between different clients.
    - Co-creation: A personal relationship is created through the customer's direct input in the final outcome of the company's products/services.
- Key Activities:
  - The most important activities in executing a company's value proposition.
  - An example for Bic would be creating an efficient supply chain to drive down costs.
- Key Resources:
  - The resources that are necessary to create value for the customer.
  - They are considered an asset to a company, which are needed in order to sustain and support the business. These resources could be
    - human,
    - financial,
    - physical

- intellectual.
- Key Partners
  - In order to optimize operations and reduce risks of a business model, organization usually cultivate buyer-supplier relationships so they can focus on their core activity.
  - Complementary business alliances also can be considered through
    - joint ventures,
    - strategic alliances between competitors or non-competitors.
- Cost Structure:
  - This describes the most important monetary consequences while operating under different business models.
  - Classes of Business Structures:
    - Cost-Driven: This business model focuses on minimizing all costs and having no frills. e.g. SouthWest
    - Value-Driven: Less concerned with cost, this business model focuses on creating value for their products and services. e.g. Louis Vuitton, Rolex
  - Characteristics of Cost Structures:
    - Fixed Costs: Costs are unchanged across different applications. e.g. salary, rent
    - Variable Costs: These costs vary depending on the amount of production of goods or services. e.g. music festivals
    - Economies of Scale: Costs go down as the amount of good are ordered or produced.
    - Economies of Scope: Costs go down due to incorporating other businesses which have a direct relation to the original product.
- Revenue Streams:
  - The way a company makes income from each customer segment.
  - Several ways to generate a revenue stream:
    - Asset Sale: (the most common type) Selling ownership rights to a physical good. e.g. Wal-Mart
    - Usage Fee: Money generated from the use of a particular service e.g. UPS
    - Subscription Fees: Revenue generated by selling a continuous service. e.g. Netflix
    - Lending/Leasing/Renting: Giving exclusive right to an asset for a particular period of time. e.g. Leasing a Car
    - Licensing: Revenue generated from charging for the use of a protected intellectual property.
    - Brokerage Fees: Revenue generated from an intermediate service between 2 parties. e.g. Broker selling a house for commission
    - Advertising: Revenue generated from charging fees for product advertising.

Appendix D: Building a Business Network Worksheet

Answering these questions will help you when you define your networking needs.

1. Who are you?

2. What is your why?

3. What do you want to achieve?

4. Who is your ideal target?

5. Who can help you reach your ideal target?

6. What can you offer to others?

7. How many relationships can you manage?

Appendix E: Financial Basics Worksheet

Here is a blank Balance Sheet and Income Statement where you can work on projecting the first two time periods of your business.

Balance Sheet

	Year	Year
Assets		
Cash		
Accounts Receivable		
Land		
Total Assets		
Liabilities		
Accounts Payable		
Notes Payable		
Total Liabilities		
Equity		
Capital Stock		
Retained Earnings		
Total Equity		
Total Equity and Liabilities		

Income Statement

	Year	Year
Revenue		
Sales		
Other Revenue		
Total Revenue		
Expenses		
Cost of Goods Sold		
Sales, General & Administrative		
Research & Development		
Total Expenses		
Earnings Before Interest, Taxes, Depreciation & Amortization		
Income Taxes		
Net Income		

Appendix F: Marketing Your Brand Worksheet

List five groups of people that fit your audience below:

1.

2.

3.

4.

5.

List as many characteristics you can come up with that separate you from the competition:

Write your explanation of your brand here and then practice it with friends and family.

Phrases and descriptions employees can use when speaking with customers/clients:

Your business brand checklist of points employees should hit when speaking to customers/clients:

Your first impression you want to make:

Your last impression you would like left with the customer/client:

Creative incentive ideas:

Appendix G: Sharing Your Idea Worksheet

For this session you will prepare a three-minute presentation about a component of your business. This means giving an example from some part or component of your businesses.

For example, an image consultant might tell someone how to put on make-up or how best to organize their closet, or a security business it might instruct a company on where to put security cameras inside the building or how to decide where lights should go outside the building. If you are building catering business, you might explain how you would you help a customer determine how much food to order for an event or how to select the appropriate menu for an event.

Consider **your** business and determine what component, piece or aspect of the business you will want to talk about. Once you've decided this, answer the following:

The purpose of your talk, speech or presentation:

Your primary audience:

Will you use visual aids to assist your presentation?

What will you want people to know or do after they've heard you?

Don't panic or avoid this – it just practice. Above all pick something you're familiar with and will enjoy talking about. Remember, you will know more about the topic than anyone else, so have fun with it!

Notes

www.ingramcontent.com/pod-product-compliance
Lightning Source LLC
Chambersburg PA
CBHW080836180526
45168CB00006B/2702